# micrographica

by renee french

ISBN 978-1-891830-93-8
1. mammals
2. humor
3. graphic novels


published by top shelf productions, po box 1282, marietta, ga 30061-1282, usa.
publishers: brett warnock and chris staros.

visit our online catalog at:
www.topshelfcomix.com.
first printing, may 2007.
printed in canada.

for rob

chapter one

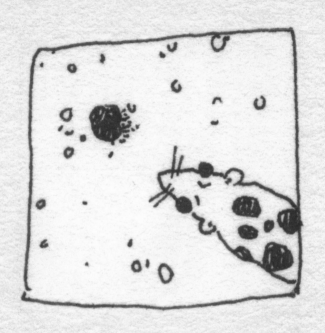

"Hmmmm."

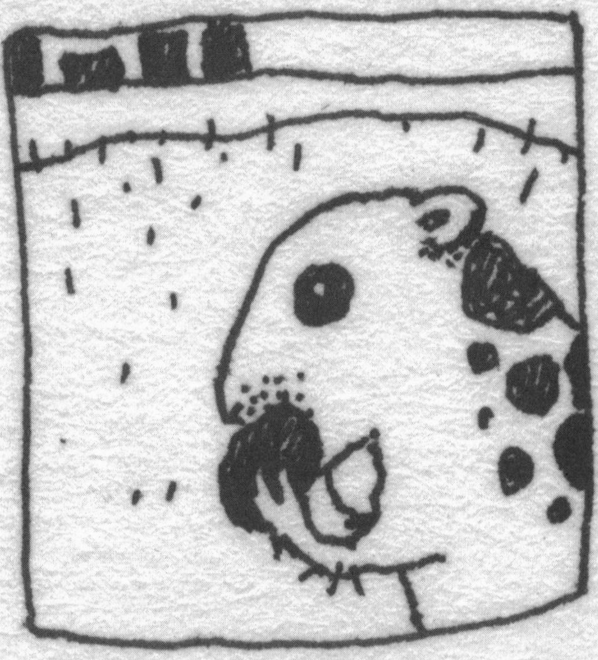

"Uh hmmmm."

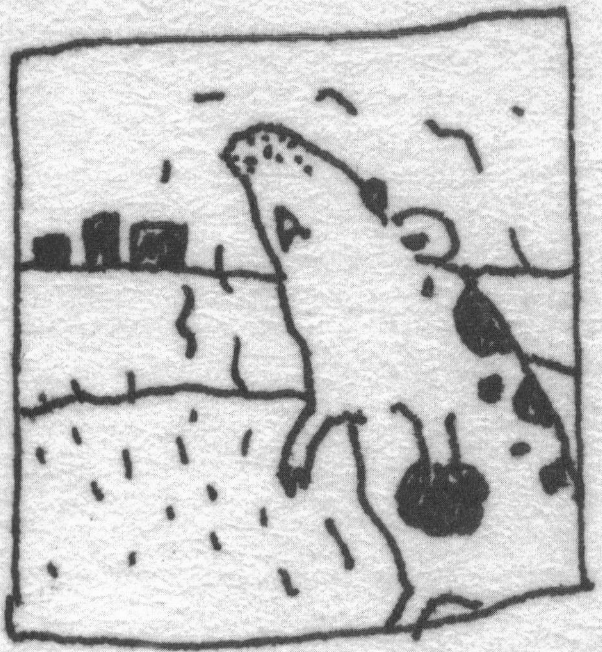

"Hey Moe, what do ya make of this?"

"Well, let me see it."

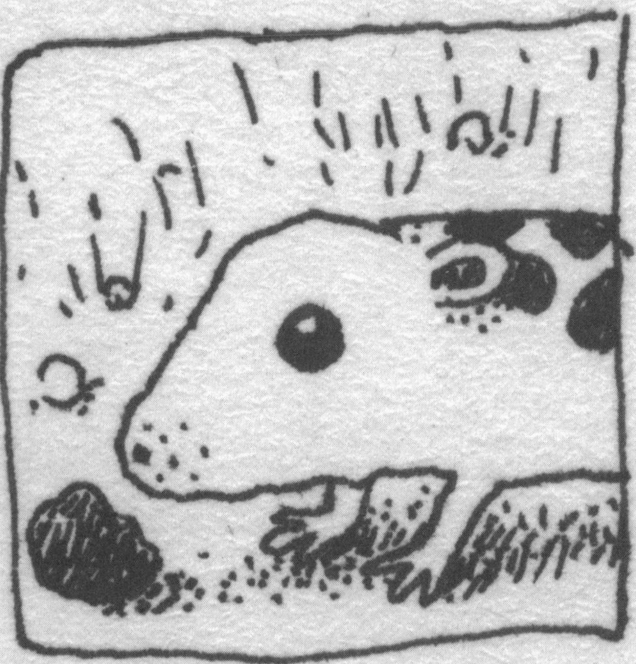

"Remember, I found it."

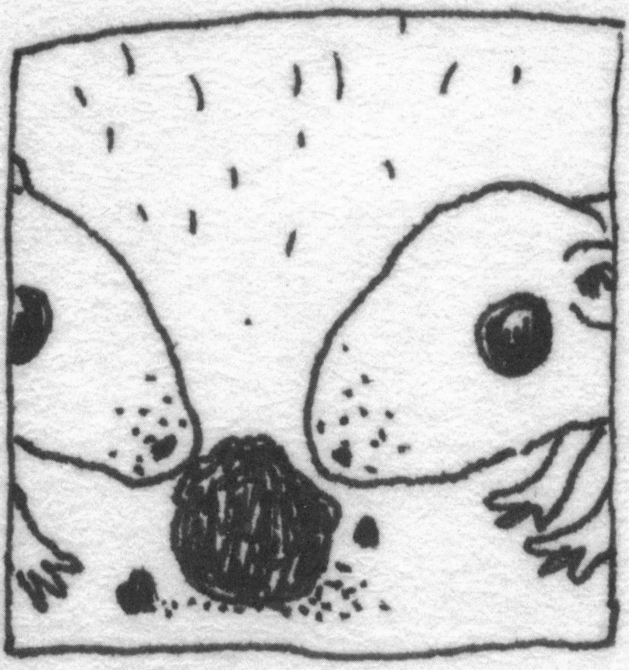

"Yeah yeah, looks like crap."

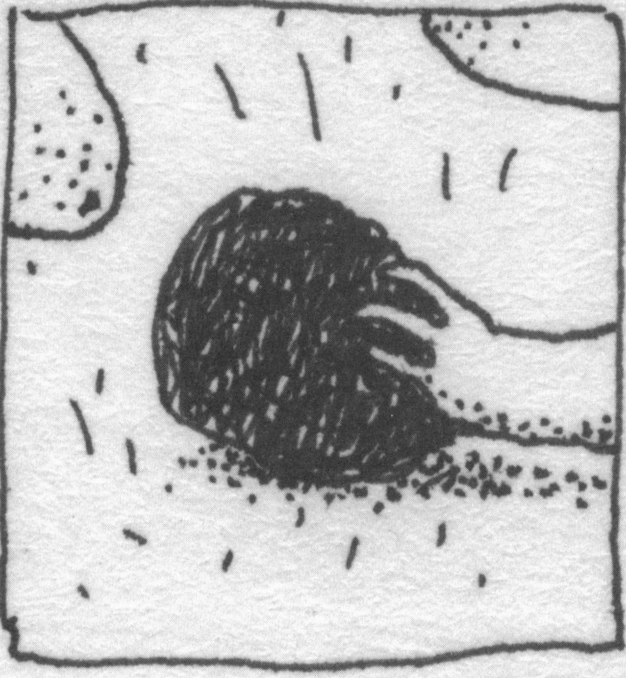

"Could be something great
wrapped in crap."

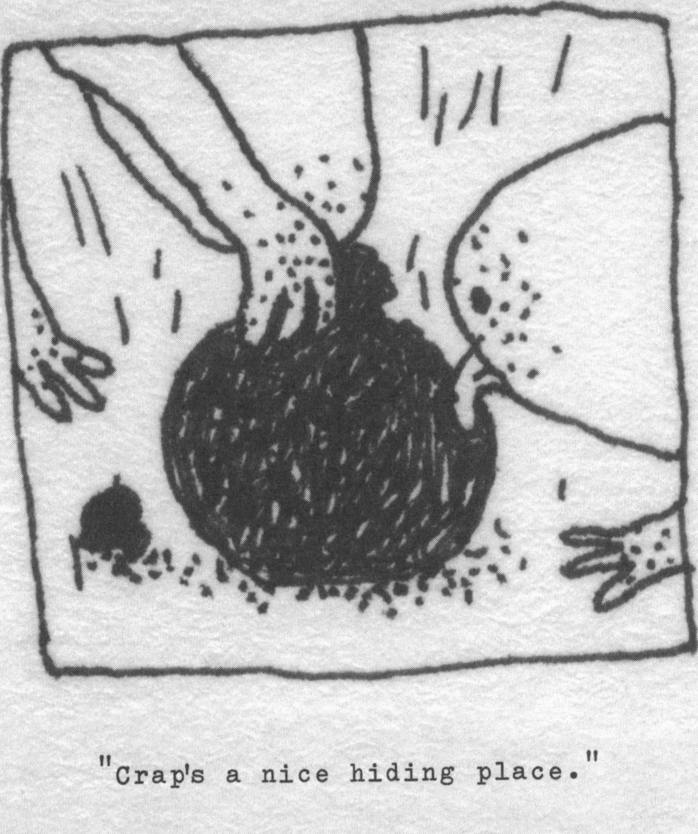

"Crap's a nice hiding place."

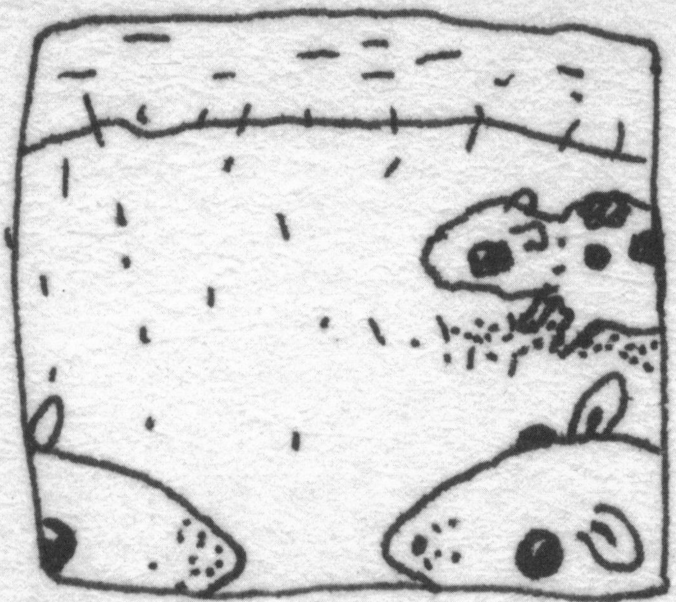

"Act natural, it's Aldo."

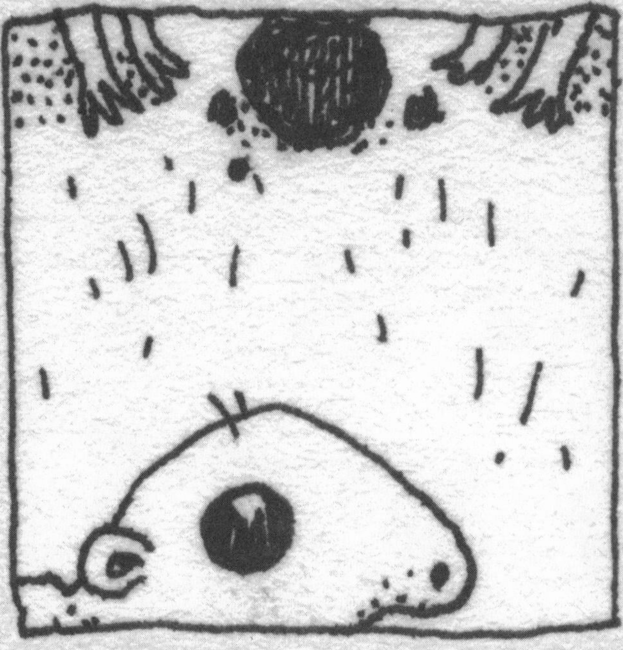

"Let him pass. Ignore the crap."

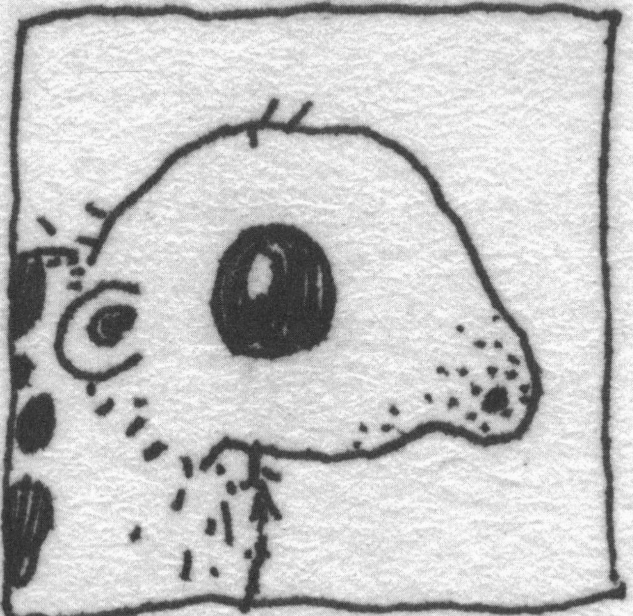

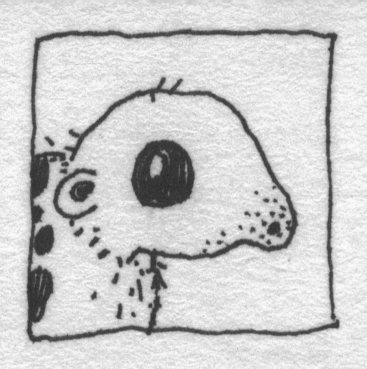

"Hi guys, whatcha up to?"

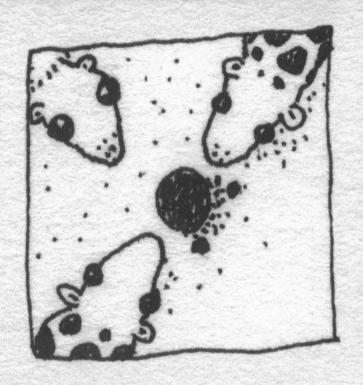

"I just found a sandwich
on Manly Beach."

"We're real jealous, Aldo."

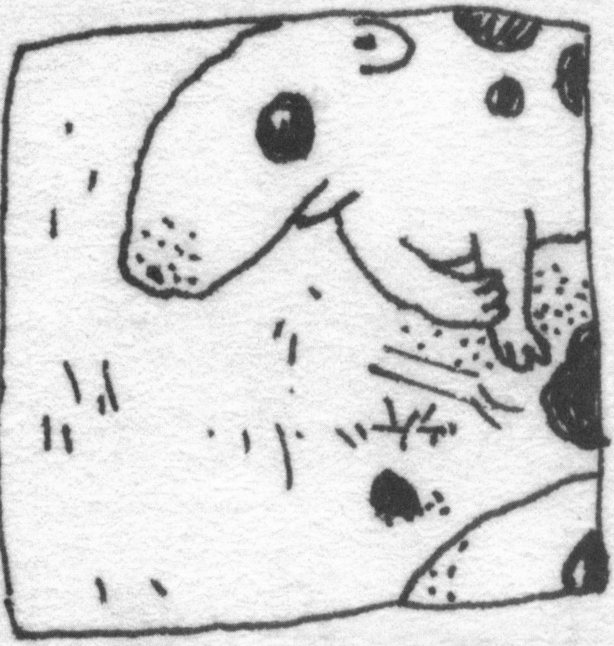

"Moe and me, we're late for a meeting."

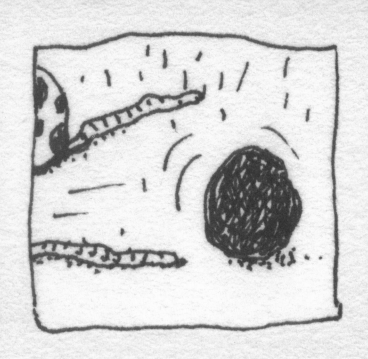

"This place is a dump."

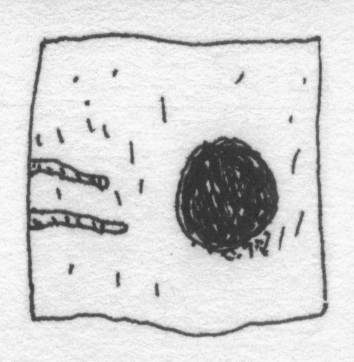

"Shh, don't look back,
just keep moving."

"Uh, ok, see you guys later."

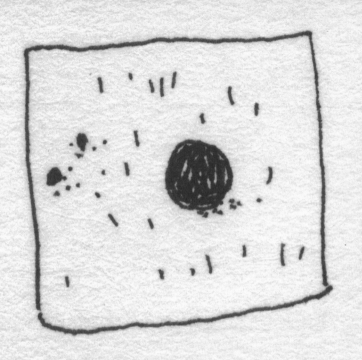

"I'll save you some sandwich."

"Hmmm. Hello there."

"Roly-poly..."

"...crapball.  Mmmmm nice."

chapter two

"Do you think that cock-knocker is
finished with our ball of crap yet?"

"Since when is it OUR ball of crap?
I found it, remember?"

"Yeah, yeah."

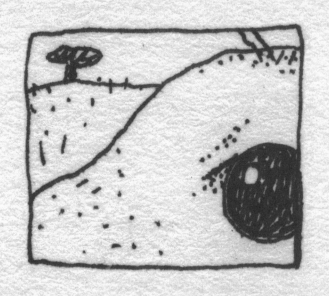

"No, I found it, Moe.  Admit it."

"Oh, this is just perfect.
You got me so upset my nose has gone
all balloony again."

"Yeah, ok, you found the crapball."

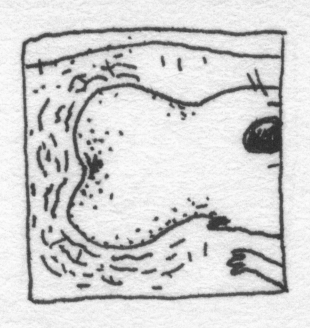

"Ow, it's pounding...wait, did you just
admit that I found the..."

"Moe?"

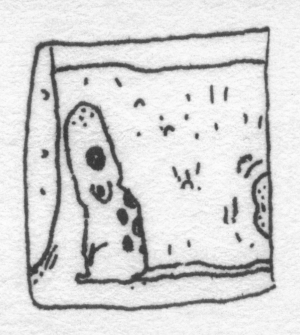

"Hey, Moe."

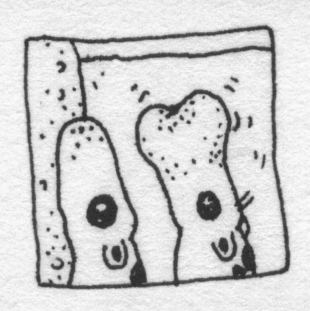

"What."

# chapter three

"What, are you crazy?
Come down from there."

"It's cinchy, C'mon."

"Maybe we should go check on Aldo
and the crapball."

"Forget about your stupid crapball."

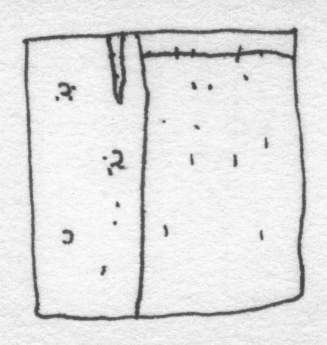

"Life was meaningless before your
Almighty Crapball."

"C'mon up.
I can see our hole from up here."

"But, my nose."

"But your nose, my ass.
You're just chicken."

"You're mean."

"Wait there then."

"Bok, bok."

"Maybe there's an easy way up
around the back."

chapter four

"Hey Moe, I think I see something."

"I think I see your crapball
from up here."

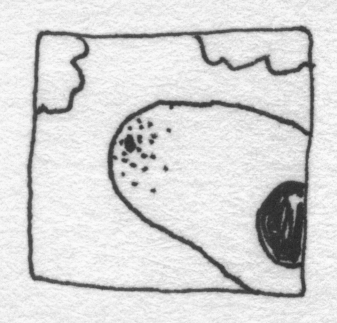

"Looks like Aldo's getting the
crapball medal of honor."

"Oh, that's so funny I forgot to
punch you in the face."

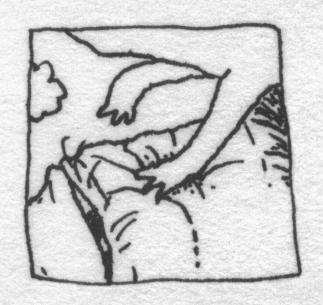

"Hey, buddy, Old pal,
there's a squishy, pouchy, thingie
up here that would be perfect
for hiding your nuts."

"Yeah, I found one too."

"Feels sorta wet
and familiar in here."

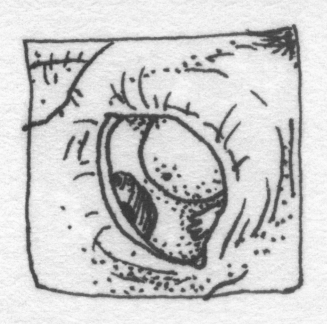

"Like your mom."

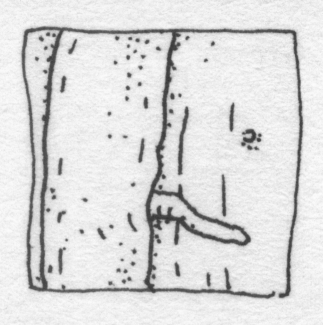

"Wet?"

"Only not as abrasive."

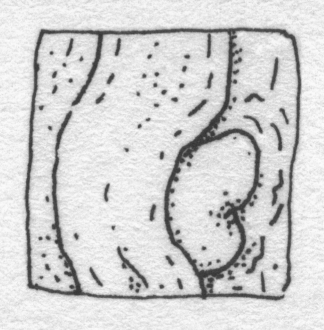

"Sniff."

"Preston?"

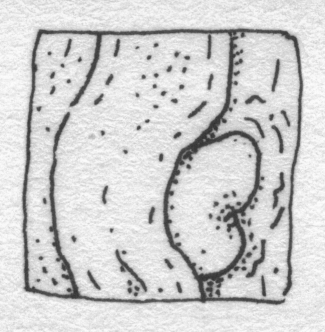

"..."

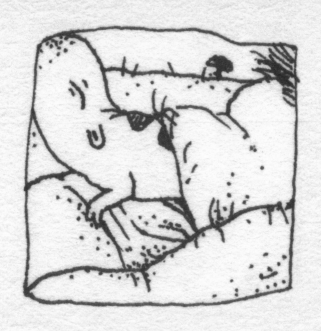

"Look, I didn't mean that thing about your mom."

"Preston...buddy?"

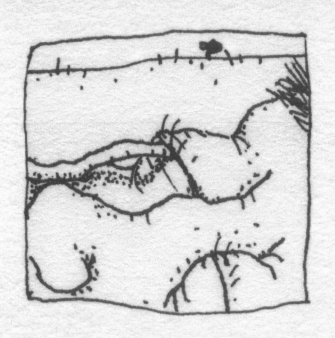

"She's not that abrasive."

# chapter five

"I wonder when the guys
are coming back."

"I don't mind being alone
with the crapball."

"But...w-w-whoah!"

"Uh oh."

"Uh."

Thwump.

"Oh, great, I broke the crapball...
I am in humongous trouble."

"Hi. I'm so sorry I broke your house.
Are you ok?"

"Can I get you something to drink,
or...eat?  You eat crap, right?"

"Maybe I should eat crap."

"OH NO!"

"Please!"

"Take me!"

chapter six

"..."

"How could I be such an idiot?"

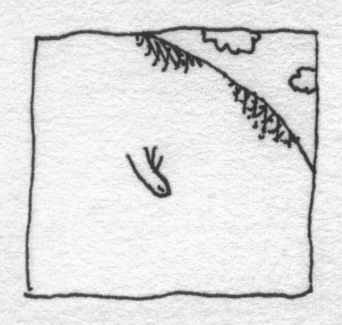

"... Hmm, what?"

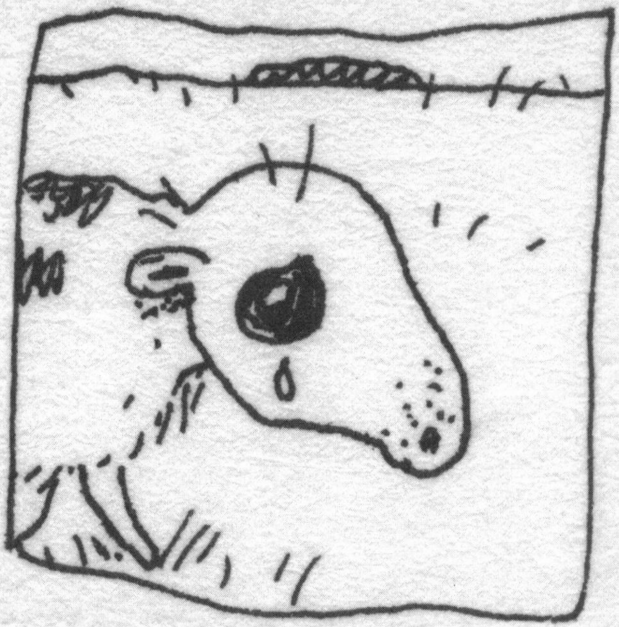

"I broke their crapball,
and now they'll never like me.
I'm such an idiot."

"Mmmm, who is this idiot?"

"Oh, that would be me."

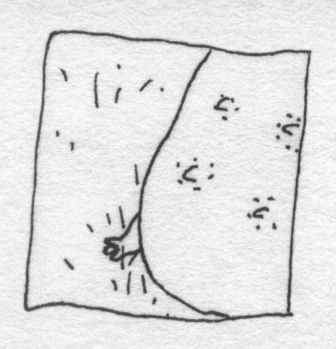

"Why do you believe you are an idiot?"

"You don't look like an idiot."

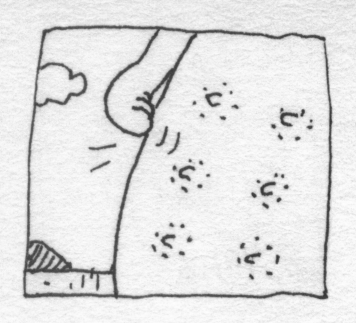

"Excuse me for just a sec, I've got eczema around my nubbins. I've been trying to scratch around the itch, not directly on the itch..."

"Uh, sorry..."

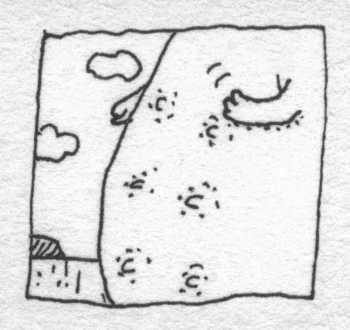

"Oh, pardon me, I was a bit
distracted. I think I'd prefer a
pain over an itch sometimes. Now, why
do you call yourself an idiot?"

"I broke my friend's crapball and now
he's going to hate me."

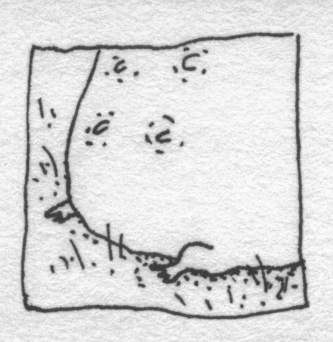

"..."

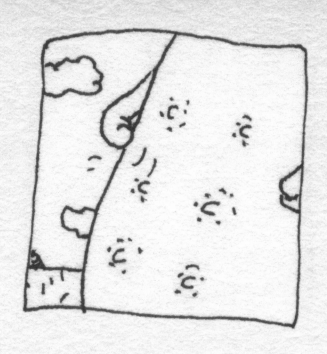

"Do you see that
brown mountain over there?"

"..."

"That brown mountain?"

"Yes."

"That mountain is a pile of crap."

"Really?"

"Oh thank you, thank you.
I'll never forget you."

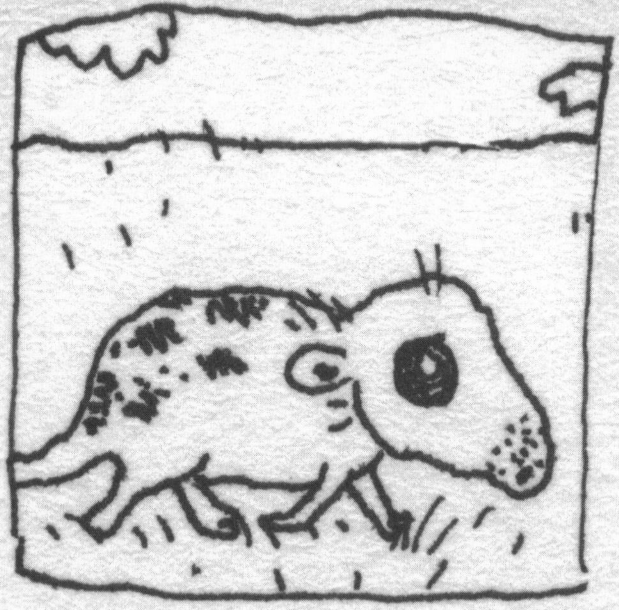

"They can't hate me if I bring them more crap than they've ever seen. Can they?"

"I wonder if he thinks
I was being literal."

chapter seven

"I really am sorry about what I
said about your mom."

"It's ok.  I know you were joking."

"Yeah, joking."

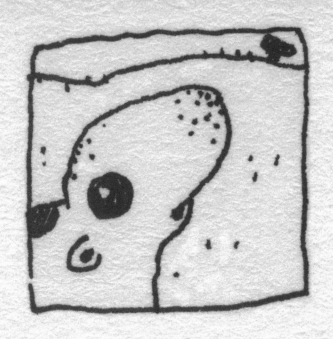

"Looks like rain."

"Could we slow down?"

"It's hard to walk with my
nose this swollen."

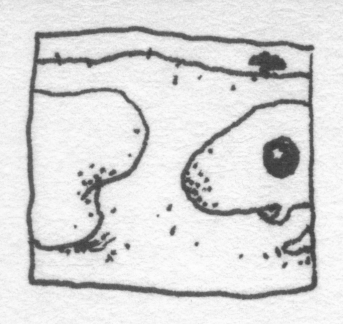

"Let me touch it, Preston.
Just a little poke."

"Maybe it's soft and yielding...
like your mom."

"Dickweed."

"I'm off to play with our crapball.
You can stay here with your nose."

"IT'S MY CRAPBALL!"

chapter eight

"Loo loo loo."

"The sky is so blue."

"The crap against the sky makes it
look even bluer."

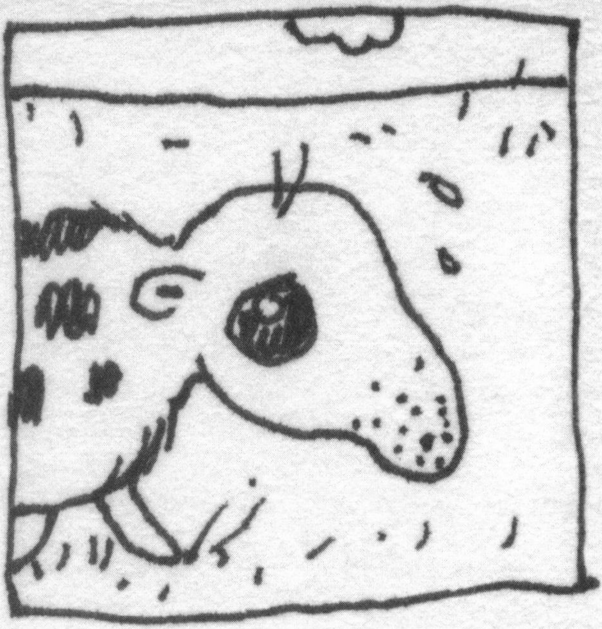

"The guys are gonna be blown away when they see my load."

"They're gonna loooooove me."

"Doo doo doo."

"I think there's a hug
coming my way."

chapter nine

"..."

"I think the swelling
is starting to go down."

"Aw, I was hoping I'd be able
to start calling you Sac-face."

"..."

"Moe, I forgot to tell you, the other
day your mom left you a message."

"Why didn't you tell me?
What did she say?"

"Pfffffffft."

chapter ten

"So dark."

"I'm ok.  It's not that cold."

chapter eleven

"It's getting dark."

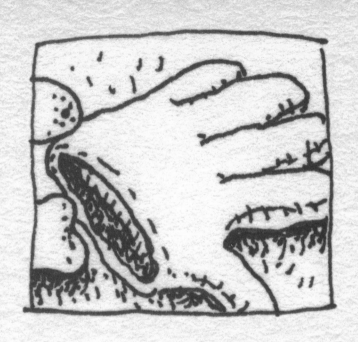

"We should camp out in this thing."

"My feet are freezing."

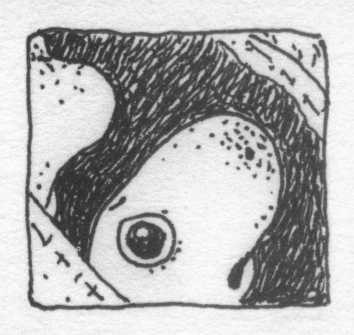

"Get your feet out of my
ass crack, Preston."

"But it's so warm."

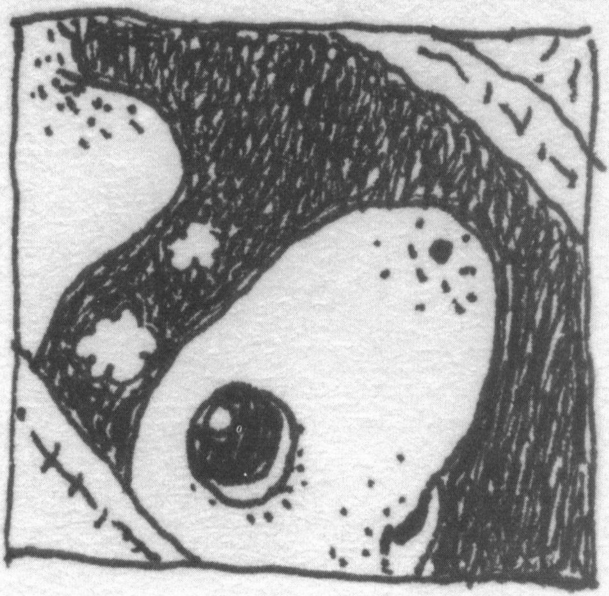

"Preston, your mom called and said to give you this...pfffffffft."

"Oh, a fart. Thanks,
it feels so warm on my toes."

"I can hear you smiling,
remove your feet from my buttocks."

"You KNOW you like it."

"I used to think you were OK, Preston,
but now I think you need to be shot in
the face every minute of every day for
the rest of your life."

"..."

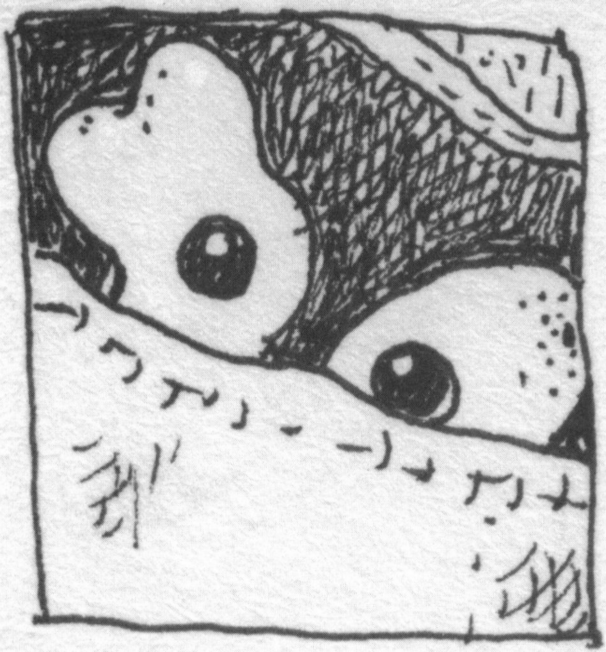

"..."

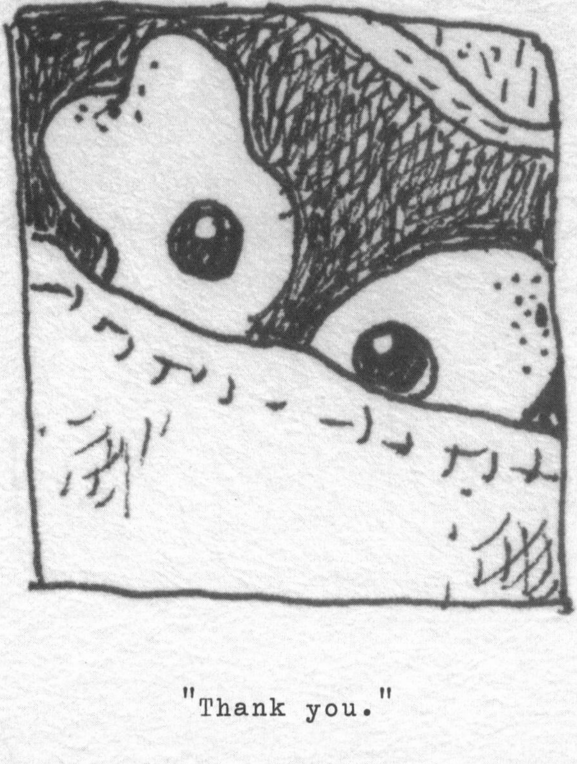

"Thank you."

"sniff."

"Preston, are you sleeping?"

"Mm hmm."

# chapter twelve

"It's not that cold."

"I'm fine."

"I'm fine."

# chapter thirteen

"I'll never get the fart smell
out of my feet, Moe."

"Hey look, a sandwich."

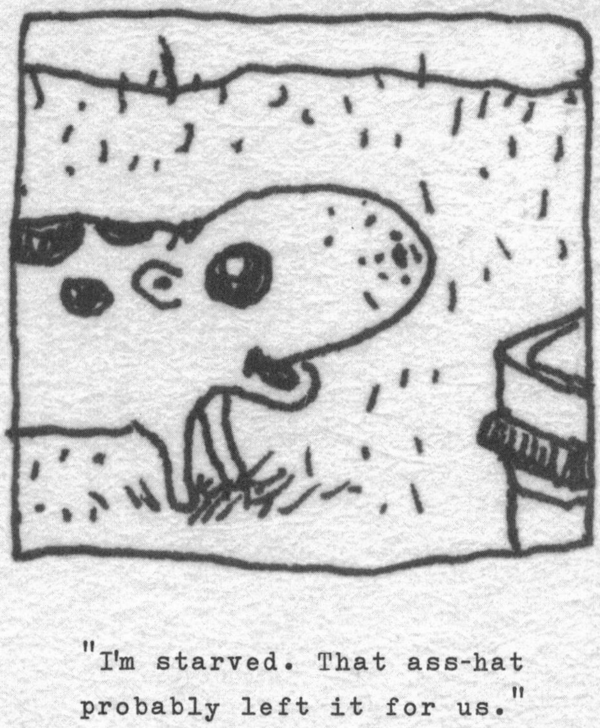

"I'm starved. That ass-hat probably left it for us."

"Yeah, I think he mentioned a sandwich he found in Manly."

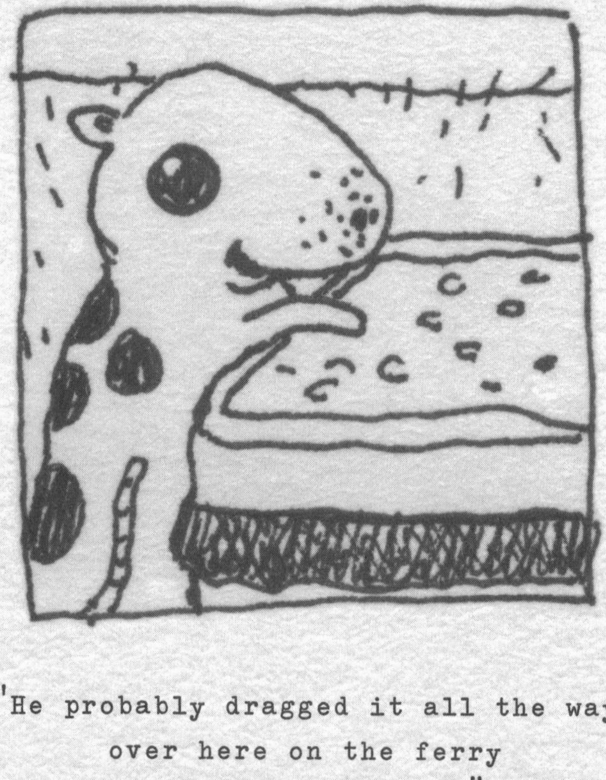

"He probably dragged it all the way
over here on the ferry
just to impress us."

"Look, my crapball!"

"This sandwich has cheese."

"It's broken. Dammit.
There's nothing inside."

"Foooey."

"Save some of that sandwich, OK?"

"What, your crapball not the center of
the universe anymore?"

"It's empty.  What's the
best part of the sandwich?"

"The seeds."

"Can I have those?"

"Sure, live it up, Sac-face."

"Hey, the swelling is down."

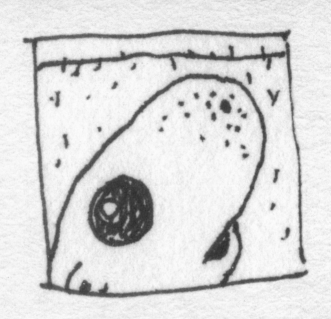

"It'll be back."

chapter fourteen

"I'm going to make it."

"I'll carry as much as I can carry."

"I can almost smell it."

"It's beautiful."

"..."

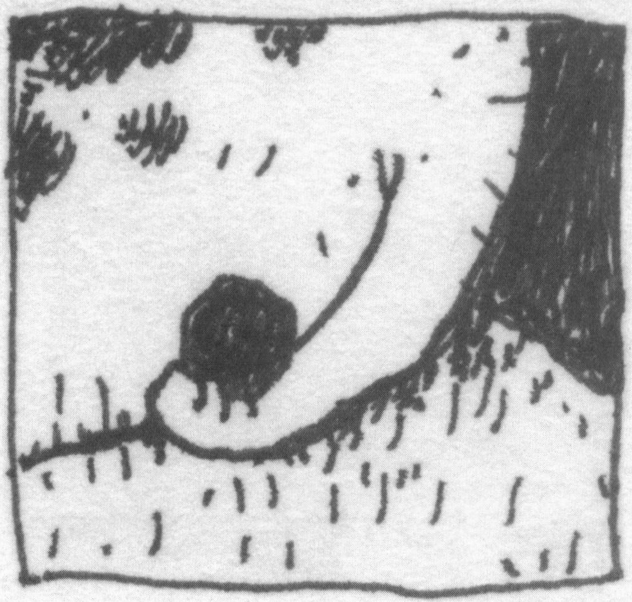

"I'm cool."

the end

The bald Mynah bird on Hunter's Hill — was ignored by the other mynah birds.

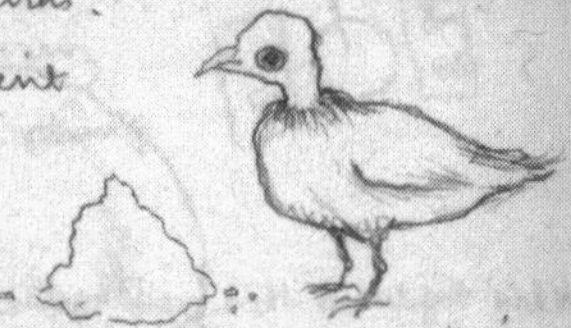

But when the others weren't looking the bald one discovered more feed than any of them had ever seen. And since it was too much to eat in one go, and since the bald one was clever, he ate enough and hid the rest under some leaves so the turtles wouldn't get it. Then he went to tell the others about his find but when he opened his mouth to tell them they turned away. So he tried again to tell them but they just ignored him as they always did. He looked at the sky and saw a Myna bird he'd never met before who landed a few feet away from him and started to talk to him about Hunter's Hill. He wanted to know what it was like living in such a nice place and so the bald one told him about the big pile of feed and they both ate some and saved some for later. The end.

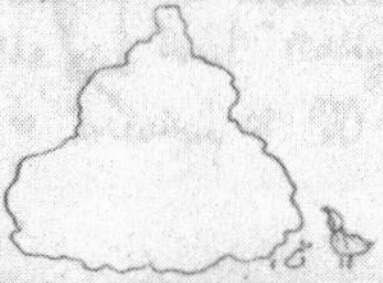

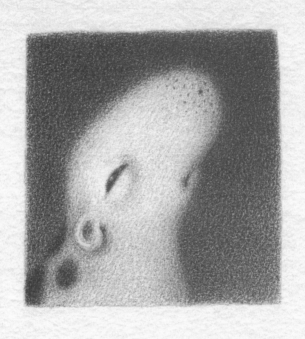

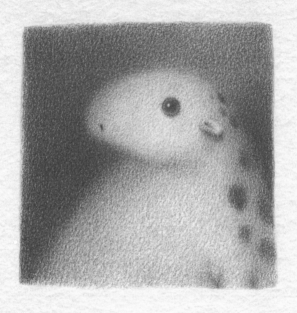

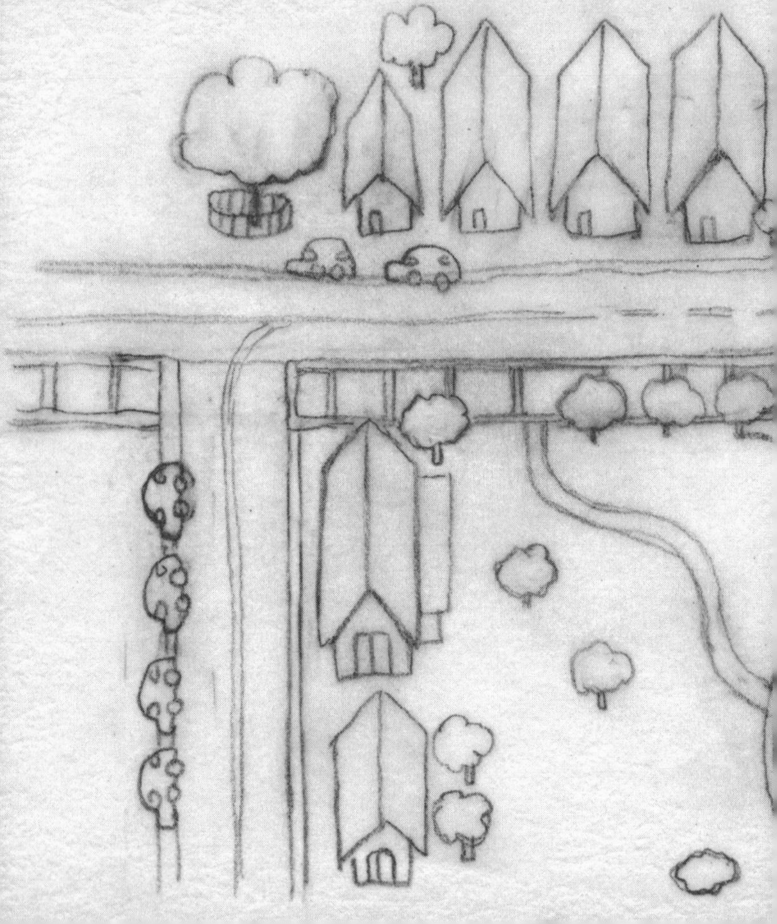

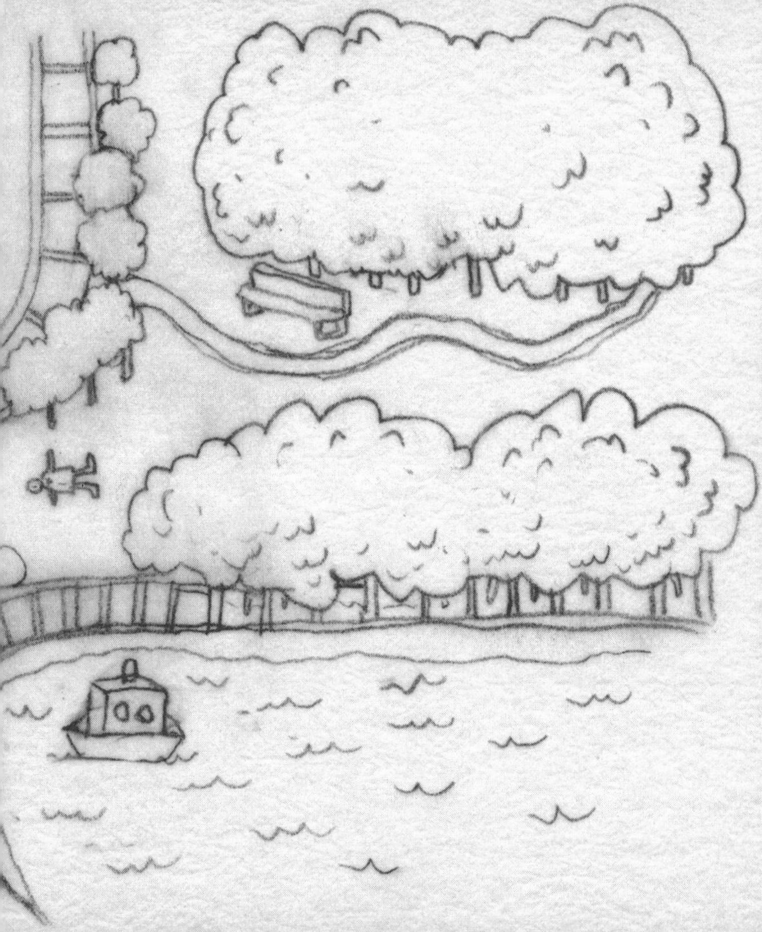

37
USA
2002

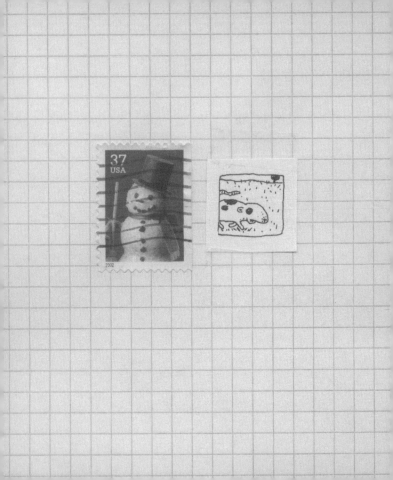

# guest crap drawings

1.

1. danny french

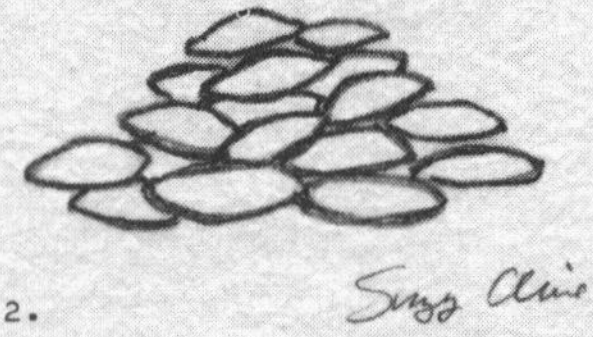
Suzy Cline

2.

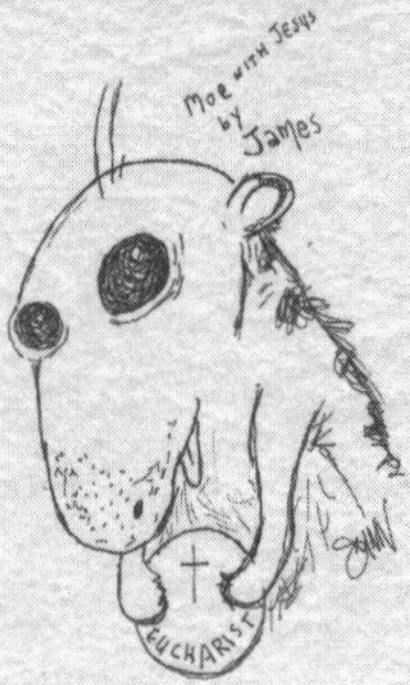
Moe with Jesus
by
James
EUCHARIST

3.

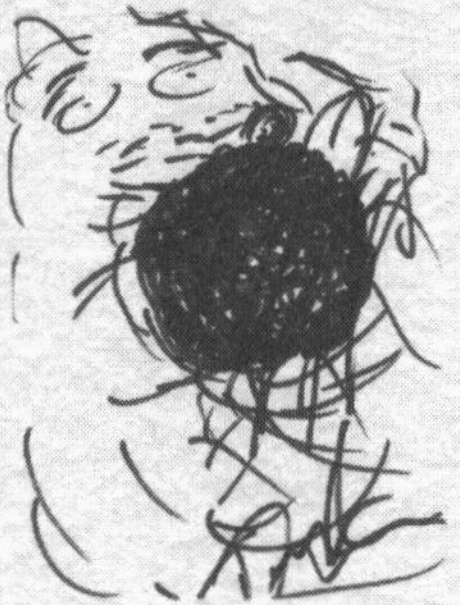

4.

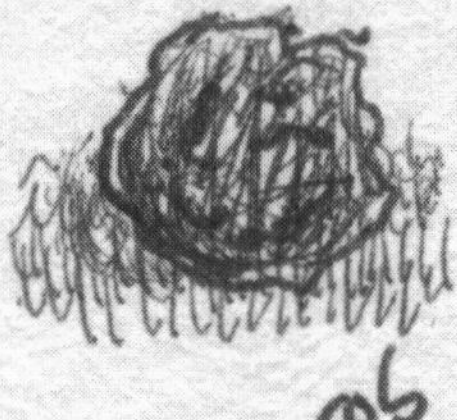
rob

5.

2. suzy cline 3. james gunn 4. dean cameron 5. rob pike

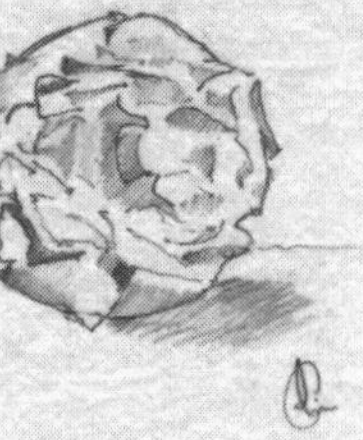

6.

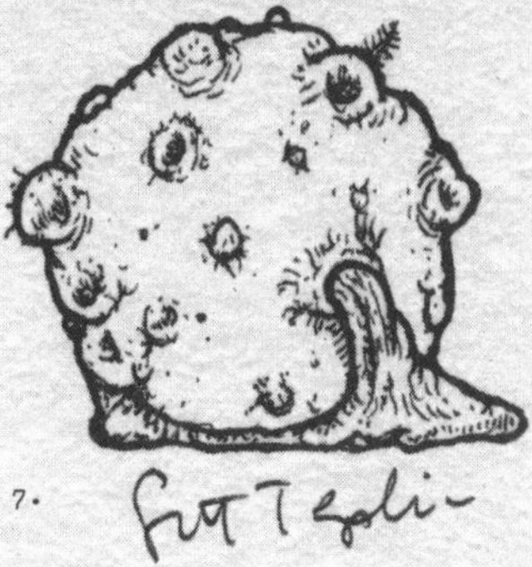

7.

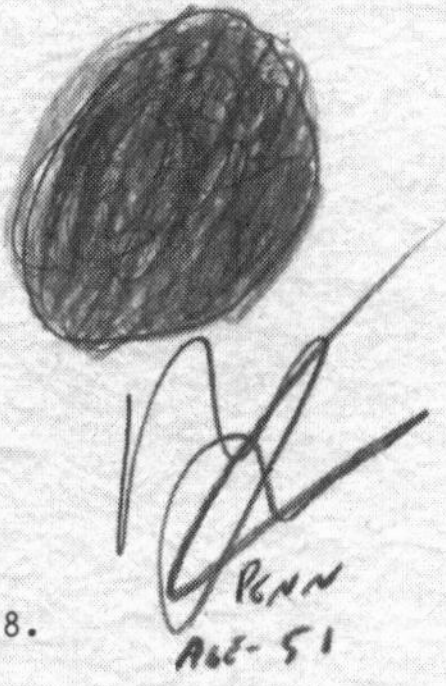
PENN
AGE- 51

8.

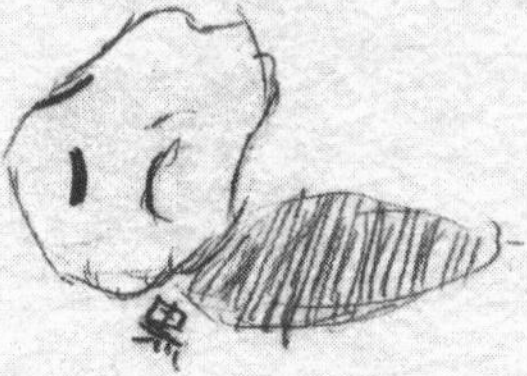

9.

6. colin summers 7. scott teplin 8. penn jillette
9. maddie holtzman

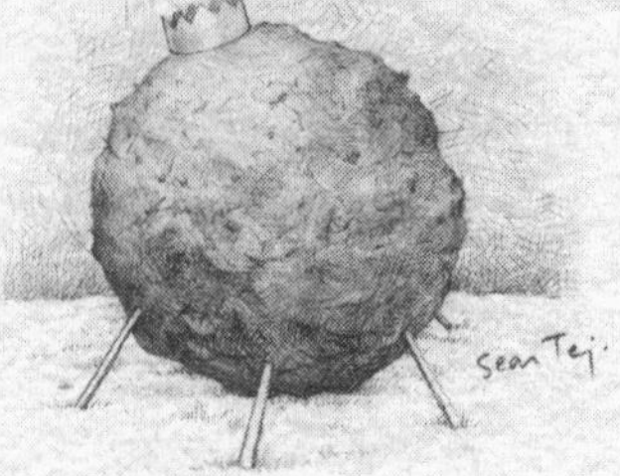
Sean Tej

10.

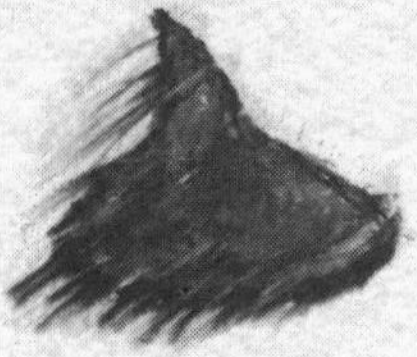

11.

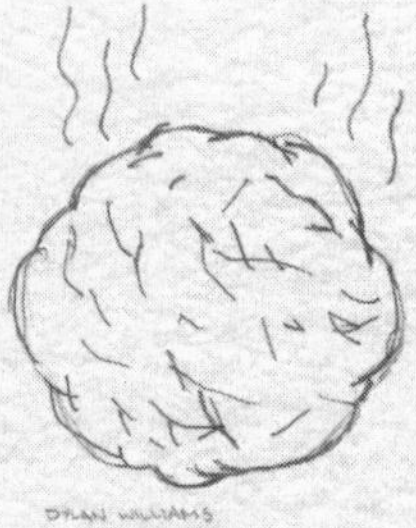
DYLAN WILLIAMS

12.

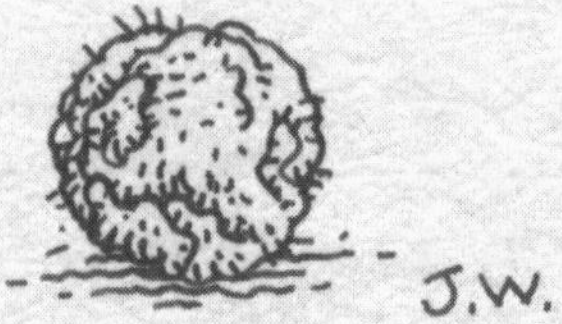
J.W.

13.

10. sean tejaratchi 11. karl hauser 12. dylan williams
13. jim woodring

thank you to:

eunice baek, ann bobco, sarah boxer, becky bregman, jeffrey
brown, shelley burnham, mike burrows, dean cameron, matt
chesse, suzy cline, jen contino, patty defrank, colman dekay,
alan david doane, anke feuchtenberger, jenna fischer, danny
french, ben fried, tom garrity, chrissy giglio, lil and bill
gladding, noel gordon, michael goudeau, james gunn, tom hart,
karl hauser, maddie holtzman, jeremyville, penn jillette, bob
and mary kersey, piers lauder, leticia macvean, joey manley,
jessie marion, jc menu, dan nadel, mark nevins, dee nicholson,
svein nyhus, rob pike, chris pitzer, paul provenza, lars
rasmussen, jamie rich, tom spurgeon, chris staros, colin summers,
sean tejaratchi, scott teplin, jane veeder, brett warnock, dylan
williams, jim woodring, and farley ziegler.